I saw the light, I saw the light
No more darkness, no more night
Now I'm so happy, no sorrow in sight
Praise the Lord, I saw the light.

HANK WILLIAMS

*H*atch Show Print has been a Nashville icon since the 1800s. Their printed posters and handbills have celebrated a wide distribution through music, political, and big-name events. Hatch Show Print continues to thrive as a working letterpress poster and design shop, creating artwork with the same printing methods they have used for more than a century.

Their interpretation of "I Saw the Light" adds visual emphasis to this journal, which carries a strong melody of encouragement and inspiration. The quotes and verses are accompanied by time-tested and much-loved graphics to make this a light-filled place to journal, sketch, or write the next big hit.

24 Hour Service

LUNCH TICKET
10¢

"Light! Give me light!" was the wordless cry
of my soul, and the light of love shone on me
in that very hour.

HELEN KELLER

24 Hour Service

LOOK!

LUNCH TICKET

God will wipe away every tear from their eyes;
there shall be no more death, nor sorrow,
nor crying. There shall be no more pain,
for the former things have passed away.

THE BIBLE

24 Hour Service

LUNCH TICKET
10c

*Into all our lives, in many simple, familiar,
homely ways, God infuses this element of joy
from the surprises of life, which unexpectedly
brighten our days, and fill our eyes with light.*

SAMUEL LONGFELLOW

N° 339

LOOKY!

LUNCH TICKET
10

It doesn't take a huge spotlight to draw attention to how great our God is. All it takes is for one committed person to so let his light shine before men, that a world lost in darkness welcomes the light.

GARY SMALLEY AND JOHN TRENT

LOOKY

24 Hour Service

LUNCH TICKET

Begin today! No matter how feeble the light,
let it shine as best it may. The world may need
just that quality of light which you have.

HENRY C. BLINN

LOOKY

Your words are what sustain me; they
are food to my hungry soul. They bring joy
to my sorrowing heart and delight me.

THE BIBLE

24 Hour Service

LOOK!

LUNCH TICKET
10¢

*No one is useless in this world who lightens
the burdens of it for another.*

CHARLES DICKENS

When faith is strong, troubles become trifles.
There can be comfort in sorrow because
in the midst of mourning, God gives a song.

No. 339

24 Hour Service

LUNCH TICKET

We're always trying to move out of the darkness,
when all we have to do is turn on the light.

Joy is more than my spontaneous expression
of laughter, gaiety, and lightness. It is deeper
than an emotional expression of happiness.
Joy is a growing, evolving manifestation
of God in my life as I walk with Him.

BONNIE MONSON

24 Hour Service

LOOK!

LUNCH TICKET

I will lead the blind by ways they have not known,
along unfamiliar paths I will guide them;
I will turn the darkness into light before them
and make the rough places smooth.

THE BIBLE

Sunshine is a matter of attitude.

F. W. BOREHAM

....

....

....

....

....

....

....

....

....

....

....

....

....

....

....

....

....

....

....

....

....

24 Hour Service

LOOK!

LUNCH TICKET
10c

God has promised strength for the day,
rest for the labor, light for the way,
grace for the trials, help from above,
unfailing sympathy, undying love.

ANNIE JOHNSON FLINT

LOOK!

LUNCH TICKET
10¢

The truly happy people are those who have a source of happiness too deep to be seriously disturbed by ordinary troubles.

MARION K. RICH

The way may at times seem dark,
but light will arise, if you trust in the Lord,
and wait patiently for Him.

ELIZABETH T. KING

*Come to me, all you who are weary
and burdened, and I will give you rest.*

THE BIBLE

LOOKY!

24 Hour Service

LUNCH TICKET
10c

A word of encouragement to those we meet,
a cheerful smile in the supermarket, a card
or letter to a friend, a readiness to witness when
opportunity is given—all are practical ways
in which we may let His light shine through us.

ELIZABETH B. JONES

N.º 339

24 Hour Service

LOOK!

LUNCH TICKET
10c

Now, God be praised, that to believing souls
gives light in darkness, comfort in despair.

24 Hour Service

LOOK!

To whistle in the dark...demonstrate[s],
if only to ourselves, that not even the dark
can quite overcome our trust in the ultimate
triumph of the Living Light.

FREDERICK BUECHNER

....
....
....
....
....
....
....
....
....
....
....
....
....
....
....
....
....
....
....

24 Hour Service

LOOK!

LUNCH TICKET

The LORD opens the eyes of the blind.

THE BIBLE

LOOKY!

LUNCH TICKET

We can be assured of this: God, who knows all and sees all, will set all things straight in the end. Even better, He will dry every tear. In the meantime He mysteriously takes our sorrows and uses them.

RICHARD FOSTER

No. 339

24 Hour Service

LOOKY!

LUNCH TICKET
10c

*Open wide the windows of our spirits
and fill us full of light.*

CHRISTINA ROSSETTI

. . . .

. . . .

. . . .

. . . .

. . . .

. . . .

. . . .

. . . .

. . . .

. . . .

. . . .

. . . .

. . . .

. . . .

. . . .

. . . .

. . . .

. . . .

. . . .

. . . .

24 Hour Service

LOOK!

LUNCH TICKET
10¢

*I believe that God is in me as the sun
is in the color and fragrance of a flower—
the Light in my darkness, the Voice
in my silence.*

HELEN KELLER

N⁰ 339

LOOK!

Grace comes into the soul, as the morning
sun into the world; first a dawning,
then a light; and at last the sun
in his full and excellent brightness.

THOMAS ADAMS

24 Hour Service

LOOK!

LUNCH TICKET
10c

His life is the light that shines through the darkness—and the darkness can never extinguish it.

THE BIBLE

LOOK!

Someday all you'll have to light the way will
be a single ray of hope—and that will be enough.

KOBI YAMADA

*No one need be downcast, for Jesus
is the joy of heaven, and it is His joy
to enter into sorrowful hearts.*

FREDERICK W. FABER

....
....
....
....
....
....
....
....
....
....
....
....
....
....
....
....
....
....

24 Hour Service

LOOK!

LUNCH TICKET
10¢

Lord, let the glow of Your love
Through my whole being shine...
Lord, make Your light in my heart
Glow radiant and clear, never to part.

MARGARET FISHBACK POWERS

24 Hour Service

LOOKY!

*God is every moment totally aware of
each one of us. Totally aware in intense
concentration and love.... No one passes
through any area of life, happy or tragic,
without the attention of God.*

EUGENIA PRICE

LOOKY

24 Hour Service

LUNCH TICKET

*The path of the righteous is like
the light of dawn, shining brighter
and brighter until midday.*

THE BIBLE

LOOKY!

LUNCH TICKET

Sometimes our light goes out but is blown into flame by another human being. Each of us owes deepest thanks to those who have rekindled this light.

ALBERT SCHWEITZER

LOOKY!

24 Hour Service

LUNCH TICKET
10¢

The best reason to pray is that God is really there. In praying, our unbelief gradually starts to melt. God moves smack into the middle of even an ordinary day.

EMILY GRIFFIN

★
★
★

LOOK!

To build in darkness does require faith.
But one day the light returns and you discover
that you have become a fortress which is
impregnable to certain kinds of trouble;
you may even find yourself needed
and sought by others as a beacon in their dark.

OLGA ROSMANITH

LOOKY

*In darkness there is no choice. It is light
that enables us to see the differences between
things; and it is Christ who gives us light.*

AUGUSTUS W. HARE

No. 339

· ·
· ·
· ·
· ·
· ·
· ·
· ·
· ·
· ·
· ·
· ·
· ·
· ·
· ·
· ·
· ·
· ·
· ·

24 Hour Service

LOOK!

LUNCH TICKET
10c

The LORD will be your everlasting light,
and your days of sorrow will end.

THE BIBLE

LOOKY!

LUNCH TICKET
10c

*It is better to light a candle
than to curse the darkness.*
    ELEANOR ROOSEVELT

100%

Trust! The way will open, the right issue will come, the end will be peace, the cloud will be lifted, and the light of eternal noonday shall shine at last.

L. B. COWMAN

LOOKY!

Time itself will in some measure heal,
and "light arises in the darkness,"
slowly, it seems, but certainly.

ELISABETH ELLIOT

LOOK

LUNCH TICKET
10¢

In all doubtful things, wait for clear light.
Look and listen for His voice and when
you are sure of it, obey.

HANNAH WHITALL SMITH

. . . .
. . . .
. . . .
. . . .
. . . .
. . . .
. . . .
. . . .
. . . .
. . . .
. . . .
. . . .
. . . .
. . . .
. . . .

24 Hour Service

LUNCH TICKET

You were once darkness, but now you are light in the Lord. Walk as children of light.

THE BIBLE

LOOK!

*Love is a happy feeling that stays inside
your heart for the rest of your life.*
                    JOAN WALSH ANGLUND

When you are in the dark, listen, and God will give you a very precious message for someone else when you get into the light.

OSWALD CHAMBERS

Abandon yourself utterly for the love of God,
and in this way you will become truly happy.

HENRY SUSO

LOOKY!

LUNCH TICKET

Life is no brief candle to me.
It is a...splendid torch...and I want
to make it burn as brightly as possible
before handing it over to future generations.

GEORGE BERNARD SHAW

Nº   339

24 Hour Service

LOOKY

LUNCH TICKET

I have tried my best to find you—don't let me wander off from your instructions.

THE BIBLE

LOOKY!

24 Hour Service

LUNCH TICKET
10c

*God's touch...lights the world with color
and renews our hearts with life.*

JANET L. SMITH

LOOK!

How could I be anything but quite happy if I
believed always that all the past is forgiven,
and all the present furnished with power,
and all the future bright with hope.

JAMES SMETHAM

24 Hour Service

LOOKY

LUNCH TICKET

But for some trouble and sorrow, we should never know half the good there is about us.

CHARLES DICKENS

LOOKY!

24 Hour Service

LUNCH TICKET
10¢

*To be blind is bad, but worse
is to have eyes and not to see.*
HELEN KELLER

24 Hour Service

LUNCH TICKET

The LORD is my light and my salvation—
whom shall I fear?
The LORD is the stronghold of my life—
of whom shall I be afraid?

THE BIBLE

24 Hour Service

LOOKY!

LUNCH TICKET
10₵

*There is a God right here in the thick of our
day-by-day lives who may not be writing
messages about Himself in the stars but in
one way or another is trying to get messages
through our blindness.*

FREDERICK BUECHNER

24 Hour Service

looky!

LUNCH TICKET
10¢

A light heart lives long.
WILLIAM SHAKESPEARE

*Begin today! No matter how feeble the light,
let it shine as best it may. The world may
need just that quality of light which you have.*

                    HENRY C. BLINN

Nº 339

LOOKY

As we let our own light shine, we unconsciously
give other people permission to do the same.
As we are liberated from our own fear,
our presence automatically liberates others.
                    MARIANNE WILLIAMSON

LUNCH TICKET

Let your light shine before others,
that they may see your good deeds
and glorify your Father in heaven.
                        THE BIBLE

N.º 339

Faith in small things has repercussions
that ripple all the way out. In a huge,
dark room a little match can light up the place.

JONI EARECKSON TADA

LOOK!

Perhaps He sees that the best waters for you
to walk beside will be raging waves of trouble
and sorrow. If this should be the case, He will
make them still waters for you, and you must
go and lie down beside them, and let them
have all their blessed influences upon you.

HANNAH WHITALL SMITH

No. 339

24 Hour Service

LOOK!

LUNCH TICKET
10c

The man who has met God is not looking for something—he has found it. He is not searching for light—upon him the Light has already shined.

A. W. TOZER

....
....
....
....
....
....
....
....
....
....
....
....
....
....
....
....
....
....
....
....

24 Hour Service

LUNCH TICKET

*Someone speaks a word of hope
to a discouraged soul, and light
shines in his prison.*

RUTH ANN POLSTON

LOOKY
!

I pray that the eyes of your heart may be enlightened in order that you may know the hope to which [God] has called you.

THE BIBLE

LOOK!

24 Hour Service

LUNCH TICKET

God's Word acts as a light for our paths.
GARY SMALLEY AND JOHN TRENT

N.º   339

LUNCH TICKET
10¢

24 Hour Service

LOOK!

One taper lights a thousand,
Yet shines as it has shone;
And the humblest light may kindle
A brighter than its own.

HEZEKIAH BUTTERWORTH

LOOK!

*You have to look for the joy. Look for the
light of God that is hitting your life, and you
will find sparkles you didn't know were there.*

BARBARA JOHNSON

24 Hour Service

LUNCH TICKET
10¢

Why should we live halfway up the hill and swathed in the mists, when we might have an unclouded sky and a radiant sun over our heads if we would climb higher and walk in the light of His face?

MACLAREN ALEXANDER

No. 339

★
★
★

LOOK!

Then they cried out to the LORD in their trouble,
and he brought them out of their distress.
He stilled the storm to a whisper;
the waves of the sea were hushed.

THE BIBLE

LOOK!

Even if your efforts seem for years to be
producing no result, one day a light that is in
exact proportion to them will flood your soul.

SIMONE WEIL

A cloudy day is no match for a sunny disposition.
WILLIAM ARTHUR WARD

It would be easier for the sun to cease to shine
and give forth heat than for a Christian
not to send forth light; easier for the light
to be darkness than for this to be so.

JOHN CHRYSOSTOM

LOOK!

*Never fear shadows. They simply mean
there's a light shining somewhere nearby.*

RUTH E. RENKEL

· ·
· ·
· ·
· ·
· ·
· ·
· ·
· ·
· ·
· ·
· ·
· ·
· ·
· ·
· ·

24 Hour Service

LUNCH TICKET
10c

Because of our God's merciful compassion,
the Dawn from on high will visit us to shine
on those who live in darkness.

THE BIBLE

LOOKY!

*If you desire to be really happy...make God
your final and ultimate goal.*

THOMAS À KEMPIS

LOOKY!

LUNCH TICKET
10c

There is not enough darkness in all the world
to put out the light of one small candle.

ARTHUR GORDON

LOOK!

What greater happiness or higher honor
could we have than to be with God,
to be made like Him and to live in His light?

ANASTASIUS OF SINAI

....

....

....

....

....

....

....

....

....

....

....

....

....

....

....

....

....

....

....

LOOKY

24 Hour Service

LUNCH TICKET
10c

From far beyond our world of trouble and care and change, our Lord shines with undimmed light, a radiant, guiding Star to all who will follow Him—a morning Star, promise of a better day.

CHARLES HURLBURT AND T. C. HORTON

The LORD my God will enlighten my darkness.
THE BIBLE

When in doubt, do nothing, but continue
to wait on God. When action is needed,
light will come.

J. I. PACKER

Ellie Claire® Gift & Paper Expressions
Franklin, TN, 37067
EllieClaire.com
Ellie Claire is registered trademark of Worthy Media, Inc.

I Saw the Light Journal
© 2016 Hatch Show Print. Used under license, all rights reserved.
Published by Ellie Claire, an imprint of Worthy Publishing Group, a division of Worthy Media, Inc.

ISBN 978-1-60936-961-3

Stock or custom editions of Ellie Claire titles may be purchased in bulk for educational, business, ministry, fundraising, or sales promotional use. For information, please e-mail info@EllieClaire.com

Cover and interior design by Hatch Show Print | www.hatchshowprint.com

Printed in China

1 2 3 4 5 6 7 8 9 – 21 20 19 18 17 16